DADDY'S TREASURE

Written by
Dr. Jenny Lanham

Illustrated by Ahmad Sabadunya

Illustrated by Ahmad Sabadunya

Produced by Publish Pros | publishpros.com

DedicaTion

This book is dedicated with unwavering love to my son, my firstborn, my Paulie. On the day of the treasure hunt, so long ago, you touched my heart with your special daddy-son adventure. While I watched this precious engagement, I wrote my thoughts down on printer paper.

Twenty-five years later, I was missing you so much, as your time in the Navy lingered for more than five years. I decided to take a chance on retelling the memory I had locked away in my heart since you were five years old.

Thank you for allowing me to share a part of your story with all who reads it. You are one of my greatest inspirations.

To all fathers, this is an example of the impact a father has on his son and how precious memories can mold and shape a life well into the future. Thank you for raising your sons well.

1 John 2:14

This is Paul.

He loves going on adventures with his daddy,
who calls him Paulie.

One day, Daddy said, "Paulie, how would you like to hunt for buried treasure?"

"All right!" Paul yelled. "That would be great!"

Daddy said, "Okay, wait here for me while I collect our gear."

Daddy hurried outside to prepare for their hunt for treasure.

"Hmm . . ." he thought to himself. " What will we need?

A shovel, a pail to keep our findings in, and, of course, our treasure map!"

When Daddy returned, he said, "Well, Paulie, it looks like we're all set! First, we need to look at our treasure map to see where we need to go."

The eager pair headed outside
and walked five paces to the left,
just as the map instructed.

"I'll count our steps,"
Paul said.

"One, two, three,
four, FIVE!"
"Great job, Buddy!"
Daddy smiled.

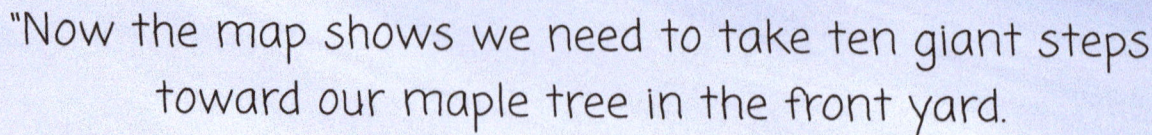

"Now the map shows we need to take ten giant steps toward our maple tree in the front yard.

Are you ready?"

"Yes, Daddy, but try to keep up!" Paul said giggling.

"Okay, funny man, let's go!" laughed Daddy.

Paul and Daddy carefully counted ten giant steps and found themselves right in front of the maple tree.

Paul asked, "Where do we go from here, Daddy?"

Daddy looked at the map.

"Well, our map says we should look for a big rock. Let me think..."

"I know, Daddy! That big rock over there, could that be it?"

"That just might be the one, Paul.
I'll race you to it!"

Daddy and Paul raced to the rock, and to their
surprise, there was a big black X on it.

"Paul, look!" Daddy pointed.

"This must be where we dig. Help me move this rock over."

"Will you start to shovel the dirt?"

Paul quickly began digging, crunching and chopping at the ground.

"Daddy, I think I am almost to the treasure!"

THUMP!
The shovel hit something, and Paul couldn't dig any further.

"Paulie!" Daddy yelled.
"I think you found the buried treasure!"

They jumped up and
down with excitement!

Daddy and Paul reached into the hole and slowly pulled up an old, wooden chest.

"I wonder what's inside.
Maybe gold or diamonds?" Paul said.

"Maybe sapphires or pearls," Daddy added.

"Well, Paulie, go ahead and open it!
Let's see what's inside!"

Paul very carefully opened the lid to the old treasure chest and could not believe what he saw inside . . .

"Paulie, what do you see?"

"It's . . . it's just an old mirror."

Paul was quite disappointed until he looked up at his daddy's face.

Daddy's eyes were sparkling with pride. Paul asked, "Daddy, are you seeing something I don't?"

"Hold up the mirror and look in it.
What do you see, Paulie?"
Paul held the mirror to his face.

"All I see is me."

"That's exactly right, son.
Look closely at your golden hair, your sapphire eyes, your
pearly white teeth, and diamond smile!

"You see Paulie,"
Daddy said lovingly,
"You are my treasure,
and there is nothing
in this world worth
more to me than
you!"

Paul thought for a moment, then held the mirror up to Daddy's face and said, "Look Daddy, I have a treasure too! I love you, Daddy."

"I love you too, Paulie."

AbOUT THE AUThOr

Dr. Jennifer Lanham earned her bachelor's degree in psychology with a focus on child psychopathology from Indiana University. She obtained a master's degree in applied behavior analysis (ABA) and a certificate in autism from Ball State University, where she also worked as an adjunct professor. Dr. Lanham completed her doctoral degree in special education at Nova Southeastern University. Her dissertation was completed and published In 2024, which focused on pica treatment for children with autism.

In 2022, Dr. Lanham opened Alphabet Soup ABA, her first clinic specializing in applied behavior analysis (ABA) for children with autism spectrum disorder, where she serves as owner, CEO, and doctorate-level board certified behavior analyst. In 2025, she opened ABS Supportive Services, providing diagnostic testing, occupational therapy, speech language pathology, and classroom-based services. That same year, she founded The Colleen Harrigan Foundation for Children with Autism.

Dr. Lanham is a resident of Indiana and has been married to Aaron Lanham for fifteen years. They have four adult children: Paul, Madison (Jennifer), Austin, and Adam (Aaron). They also have two fur babies: Steve and Bo. In her free time, Dr. Lanham spends time with family and friends and loves musical and creative endeavors.

www.ingramcontent.com/pod-product-compliance
Lightning Source LLC
Chambersburg PA
CBHW041531120626
46551CB00018B/2653